ADVANCED CURRICULUM FROM THE
CENTER FOR GIFTED EDUCATION AT WILLIAM & MARY

MATH
Curriculum
for Gifted Students

GRADE 4

Lessons, Activities, and Extensions for Gifted and Advanced Learners

Student Workbook
Sections I-II

CENTER FOR GIFTED EDUCATION
WITH MOLLY BRYAN TALBOT

William & Mary
School of Education

CENTER FOR GIFTED EDUCATION
P.O. Box 8795
Williamsburg, VA 23187

First published in 2020 by Prufrock Press Inc.

Published in 2021 by Routledge
605 Third Avenue, New York, NY 10017
2 Park Square, Milton Park, Abingdon, Oxon OX14 4RN

Routledge is an imprint of the Taylor & Francis Group, an informa business.

ISBN-13: 978-1-64632-024-0

Edited by Lacy Compton

Cover and layout design by Allegra Denbo and Shelby Charette
Printed and bound by CPI Group (UK) Ltd, Croydon, CR0 4YY

NEW YORK AND LONDON

TABLE OF CONTENTS

LESSON 1.1 ACTIVITY
Factor Pairs and Multiples

Directions: You and your partner have been selected to design patterns for artwork. Follow the directions below to complete your artwork.

- With your partner, take turns drawing a card from the deck (cards numbered 1–100).
- Using the counters, investigate to see how many arrays you and your partner can create using the number of counters designated by the card drawn.
- Record all arrays created on the graph or chart paper provided. Make sure you label the arrays with the correct length and width.

1. Using your arrays written on your graph or chart paper, record all factor pairs in the space provided below. If you have different factor pairs for the same number, be sure to discuss these differences with your partner.

My Factor Pairs	My Partner's Factor Pairs

2. Using the pile of cards drawn for the first part of this activity, you and your partner should each choose one number card from each pile and find the specified multiples of that number.

   a. My Number: _____   3rd multiple: _____

   My Partner's Number: _____   3rd multiple: _____

   b. My Number: _____   6th multiple: _____

   My Partner's Number: _____   6th multiple: _____

3. Using the hundreds chart provided, color a stripe in each box for each of the numbers that are multiples of the following numbers:

   a. 2: Color red
   b. 3: Color blue
   c. 4: Color orange
   d. 5: Color black
   e. 6: Color purple
   f. 7: Color yellow
   g. 8: Color pink

4. Discuss with your partner whether or not you can create any generalized rules to determine if a number is a multiple of another number. Write any generalized rules in the space provided.

Extend Your Thinking

1. Find numbers that create squares with their arrays. These numbers are called square numbers. See how many square numbers you can find between 1 and 100. List them in the space below.

2. Find the numbers between 1 and 100 that can create only one array, with the dimensions of 1 times that number. These are called prime numbers. Identify all of the prime numbers between 1 and 100.

LESSON 1.1
Number Cards

1	13	25	37
2	14	26	38
3	15	27	39
4	16	28	40
5	17	29	41
6	18	30	42
7	19	31	43
8	20	32	44
9	21	33	45
10	22	34	46
11	23	35	47
12	24	36	48

49	62	75	88
50	63	76	89
51	64	77	90
52	65	78	91
53	66	79	92
54	67	80	93
55	68	81	94
56	69	82	95
57	70	83	96
58	71	84	97
59	72	85	98
60	73	86	99
61	74	87	100

LESSON 1.1 PRACTICE
Factor Pairs and Multiples

Directions: Complete the problems below.

1. Sara said that the number of cars in the parking lot is a prime number, because there are an odd number of cars. Aaron disagreed and said that the number of cars in the parking lot is a composite number because they can be arranged in different arrays. The cars in the parking lot are parked like this:

    a. Who is correct? _____

    b. How do you know?

    c. How many other ways could the cars be parked to form a rectangular array?

    d. What is the minimum number of cars that would need to be added to make the number of cars in the parking lot a prime number? How do you know?

2. Tic-Tac-Tile Company is designing a kitchen for the Browning family. The Brownings have purchased enough tiles for an area of 72 square feet for their kitchen.

   a. Draw all possible array designs the Brownings could use for their kitchen, if each tile measures 1 foot by 1 foot. Use a separate sheet of paper to draw your arrays.

   b. The Brownings would like a kitchen that is as close to a square as possible. Which design should the Brownings choose? Explain your reasoning.

   c. If the Brownings wanted to change their kitchen from "close to a square" to an exact square, how many square feet would their new kitchen have if they did not want to buy more tile, yet want to keep the size as close as possible to 72 square feet? Use both words and pictures to explain your answer.

3. Write all of the factor pairs for the numbers listed below.

   36, 63

   a. Use the Venn diagram to record all factors of 36 and 63.

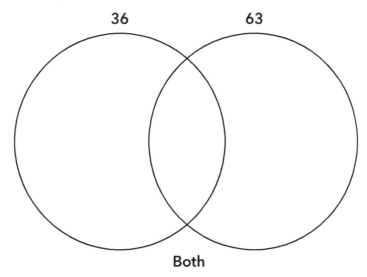

36   63

Both

b. Using the factors of 36 and 63 from the Venn diagram in Part A, generalize a rule for multiples of the number 9.

4. Test your generalizations with numbers.
   a. Is this true for 9 x 11? 9 x 12? 9 x 13? What can you say about your generalizations based on these numbers?

   b. Look at the multiples of 3, 4, and 6 to see if you can develop any other generalizations regarding multiples of these numbers.

5. Multiple madness: For the following questions, answer with the number that applies to the statement listed.
   a. Which number between 1 and 100 has only 10 fours? _____

   b. Which number between 1 and 100 has only 3 sixes? _____

   c. Which number between 1 and 100 has only 9 nines? _____

   d. Create your own multiple madness question to give to a friend.

Extend Your Thinking

1. Draw two cards from a set of number cards and compare the factor pairs of the two numbers to see if you can generalize any rules for multiples that have not been generalized already.

LESSON 1.1
Assessment Practice

Directions: Complete the problems below.

1. Mr. Beasley is buying pretzels for his snack machines. Each machine can hold 9 packs of pretzels. Assuming all of his machines are out of pretzels, which could be the total number of pretzel packs Mr. Beasley is buying?
   a. 40
   b. 85
   c. 63
   d. 56

2. Use the list of numbers below to answer the question. Which of the numbers listed are prime? Circle them.

   0, 1, 2, 3, 5, 6, 8, 9, 18, 23, 32, 49, 81, 87, 89, 99

3. Which of the following is a multiple of 4?
   a. 90
   b. 64
   c. 34
   d. 14

4. Which number below has these factor pairs?

   3 and 15, 5 and 9

   a. 45
   b. 50
   c. 36
   d. 30

LESSON 1.2 ACTIVITY
Multiplicative Comparison Scavenger Hunt

Directions: Complete the following steps on your scavenger hunt.

1. With a partner, go on a scavenger hunt around your classroom to find the following items.
    a. An item that is approximately 6 times as long as a box of crayons.

    b. An item that is approximately 5 times as wide as an unsharpened pencil is long.

    c. An item that is approximately 2 times as wide as a sheet of paper is long.

    d. An item that is approximately 2 times as wide as an index card is long.

2. Now create a tape diagram for two of your "found" items from Step 1.

3. Write an equation, using a variable for your unknown, to represent the tape diagrams you created in Step 2.

Extend Your Thinking

1. Using your knowledge of multiplicative comparison and the information found in the scavenger hunt, relate two items in your classroom using a multiplicative comparison.

2. Explain the relationship between a box of crayons and a sheet of loose-leaf paper based on your scavenger hunt information.

LESSON 1.2 PRACTICE
Multiplicative Comparison Is for the Dogs

Directions: Use the table to answer the following problems.

Dog Breed	Average Height of Breed (in.)
Cane Corso Mastiff	27 in.
Chihuahua	6 in.
Afghan Hound (female)	25 in.
Rhodesian Ridgeback	24 in.
Basenji (male)	24 in.
Dachshund	5 in.
Brussels Griffon	7 in.
Yorkie	8 in.

1. Compose three word problems that show evidence of multiplicative comparison. For your word problems, include at least one problem that shows an unknown product, one problem that shows group size unknown, and one problem that shows number of groups unknown.

2. For each word problem you composed above, draw a tape diagram that would accurately represent each comparison in the word problem.

3. For the tape diagrams you drew above, write an equation that would accurately represent each. Remember to use a variable to represent your unknown in each problem.

4. Jackie was a judge at the dog show. She had to judge one group of 65 dogs the first round. During the second round, she had to judge a group of 13 dogs. How many times more dogs did Jackie judge in the first round than the second round?

   _____

5. In the second round, the dogs were divided into groups of small dogs and large dogs, so she had one group of 5 small dogs and one group of 8 large dogs to compose the group of 13 dogs. What type of comparison is seen in this group that is different than the comparison that is seen between the first-round and second-round groups?

Extend Your Thinking

1. Research some famous monuments around the world. Compare the heights or widths of these monuments to an item in your classroom.

LESSON 1.2
Assessment Practice

Directions: Complete the problems below.

1. 56 is eight times as many as which number?
   a. 5
   b. 6
   c. 7
   d. 8

2. It takes Joey four times longer than Megan to get to school. It takes Megan 6 minutes to get to school. How long does it take Joey to get to school?
   a. 4 minutes
   b. 6 minutes
   c. 12 minutes
   d. 24 minutes

3. Boris has 72 stamps in his collection. He has eight times as many stamps as his friend Jane. How many stamps does Jane have?
   a. 6
   b. 7
   c. 8
   d. 9

4. Ari waited in line for the roller coaster eight times longer than she waited in line for the fun house. She waited 96 minutes to ride the roller coaster. Write an equation that shows how to find the number of minutes Ari waited in line for the fun house. Then solve the equation.

5. A bookshelf is 60 inches tall. The bookshelf is four times taller than the table beside it. Write an equation to show what you would need to do in order to find the height of the table.

Math Curriculum for Gifted Students, Grade 4, Sections I–II

LESSON 1.3 ACTIVITY I
Traveling Through Numbers

Directions: Complete the steps below.

1. Think of a place you have always wanted to visit within the U.S. Write this in the table below.

2. Use a map or a website such as Google Maps to determine how far your destination is from your school. Write the miles in the table below.

3. Because you want to be safe on your trip, you decide to only drive a total of 12 hours per day. Determine how many days your trip will take and write this in the table below.

4. Now, draw a travel card to see what type of vehicle you will be driving, average gas mileage of your vehicle, and the fuel tank capacity of your vehicle. Write this information in the table below.

Traveling Through Numbers Checklist

❑ Departure city _____

❑ Destination city _____

❑ Fuel you began with (assume you had a full tank) _____

❑ Miles to destination _____

❑ Days trip will take _____

❑ Miles traveled each day _____

❑ Miles to gallon used in your vehicle _____

❑ Evidence of the four mathematical operations to be used to find the answer of your problem

❑ Evidence of estimation strategies used to find an estimated answer, not a precise answer

---

5. Using the information in Steps 1-4, develop a word problem that estimates how many gallons of gas you would need to make a round trip to your destination that meets all of the criteria listed in the checklist on page 15. Be sure to include your answer to your word problem.

6. Now, swap your word problem with a partner. Your partner will need to determine the best estimation strategies to solve the word problem in order to arrive at the same estimated answer.

Extend Your Thinking

1. Ask your parents about a trip you have taken as a family in your family vehicle (or a trip you would like to take if you have not actually gone on one). Write a multistep word problem regarding this trip and trade it with a classmate.

LESSON 1.3
Travel Cards

Chevrolet Tahoe

26-gallon tank

Average of 21 miles per gallon

GMC Yukon

31-gallon tank

Average of 21 miles per gallon

Ford Expedition

26-gallon tank

Average of 18 miles per gallon

Subaru Forester

15-gallon tank

Average of 27 miles per gallon

LESSON 1.3 ACTIVITY II
Interpreting Remainder Memory Match

Directions: Complete the steps below.

1. Take turns with a partner turning two cards over at a time. Make sure to keep the cards in the same location (do not pick them up; simply turn them over).

2. Look at the cards to decide if the best method for interpreting the remainder matches for each card. If the method needed to interpret the remainder matches on both cards, that person gets to keep the cards.

3. Play continues until players take all cards.

Extend Your Thinking

1. Look at the cards you have in your pile. There are extension questions at the bottom of each card. Complete these as best you can!

LESSON 1.3

Interpreting Remainder Memory Match Cards

Thomas, Julia, Calla, Jonas, Gabriela, and James received a bag of Airheads as a prize for their winning science project. The bag contained 31 Airheads. They know that each of them can get 5 whole Airheads and 1/6 of the remaining Airhead.

Extension: Write the division problem for the word problem written above.

a

There was enough water remaining in the container for each player on the football team to get 4.5 cups of water during the second half of the game.

Extension: How much water was in the cooler at the beginning of the game if there were 12 players on the team and each player had already had 3 cups of water before halftime?

b

Evangelina was making cupcakes for an event at school. She needed one for each person in her class of 25 people. Each pan could make 12 cupcakes. Because she had extra, she was able to eat a cupcake herself.

Extension: If she needed to triple the number of cupcakes for the event, how many batches of cupcakes would she have to bake, assuming that she had only one baking pan?

c

William needed 4 feet of rope to complete three complicated knots in order to earn a badge in his club. He found a rope in his dad's shed that measured 4.8 feet. He left his dad the remaining 0.8 feet of the rope.

Extension: About how much of the rope could be used for each knot if all three of the knots were the same in length?

d

Your favorite action figures are on sale at the store for $13.99 each instead of the regular price of $19.99 each. You have $84 that you have been saving. You know you can buy 6 action figures and still have $0.06 remaining.

Extension: Explain how you could have arrived at your answer using both pictures and words.

e

You and 4 friends want to evenly split the flowers you gathered this afternoon in the meadow. You picked 47 flowers, so each person can get 9 flowers and there will be 4 flowers remaining.

Extension: How many more flowers would need to be picked for each person to have 12 flowers?

f

The school was taking 4 classes on a field trip, with a total of 84 students going. Each van can hold 13 students. The school knows that they will need 7 vans to get all students to the field trip.

Extension: If the whole school of 348 students went on the field trip, how many vans would they need then?

g

Yasmine is placing mats out for a tumbling class. She knows that there are 57 students in her next class and that she can put 7 students on a mat. She knows she will need 9 mats total to accommodate all of the students.

Extension: If she wanted to put 3 students on each mat instead, how many mats would she need?

h

LESSON 1.3 PRACTICE
Remainders and Estimation

Directions: Complete the problems below.

1. For the homecoming parade, each class brought in bags of candy. The total number of pieces of candy brought by each class is shown in the table.

Class	Number of Pieces of Candy Brought
Mr. Plauche's class	482
Mr. Dayton's class	543
Ms. Manuel's class	526
Mrs. Sample's class	547
Mr. Stagg's class	471

A few students made estimates on the total number of pieces of candy the school had collected. Their estimations are shown below. Use their estimation, the chart above, and your knowledge of estimation strategies to answer A–C.

Claire = 2,550 pieces   Parker = 2,500 pieces   Cora = 2,476 pieces

a. What estimation strategy did each person use to determine their answer? Explain using words.

b. Explain how Cora and Parker could use two different estimation strategies and end up with the same sum.

c. Who would have the most reasonable estimation if the school needed to determine if there would be enough candy for each of the 10 floats in the parade to have 400 pieces of candy to throw?

2. Read each of the following division problems. Explain what you would do with the remainders in each problem and why you would do this, and then state the final answer to each problem.

   a. Katie invites 7 of her friends to her party. She wasn't sure how many would show up, so she made 60 cupcakes just in case. If all of the people at the party, including Katie, have an equal share of the cupcakes, how many cupcakes will they get if they share every last bit?

   b. The school is having a parent meeting and is expecting 60 parents to show up. There is room in the auditorium for rows of 8 chairs each. If parents fill in starting in the front rows first, how many seats will be empty in the partially filled last row?

   c. It's time for the state fair, and Farmer Brown is sending 60 pigs to be sold. He will transport the pigs in small trailers that can hold 8 pigs each. How many trailers will he need?

3. Your mom is helping with a school fundraiser. She ordered 30 packs of plastic eggs, with each pack containing 12 eggs. The school had already donated 15 packs of these plastic eggs. Your mom knows she needs around 640 eggs to be evenly divided between the 9 booths for the fundraiser.

   a. How many more packs are needed to make sure she has about 640 total eggs? _____ Explain how you arrived at your answer.

   b. How many eggs will each booth get? _____
   c. What would you suggest your mom does with the remainder?

4. Write different word problems involving 88 ÷ 5 = ?, where the answers are best represented as:

   a. 17

   b. 17 r 3

   c. 18

   d. 17 or 18

   e. $17\frac{1}{2}$

Extend Your Thinking

1. Use a calculator to see if you can determine any patterns with divisors and patterns with remainders.

LESSON 1.3
Assessment Practice

Directions: Complete the problems below.

1. Presleigh is playing a video game.
   - After she found the hidden treasure, her score doubled.
   - After she stepped on the lily pad, she lost 10 points.
   - Presleigh's new score is 80 points.

   How many points did Presleigh have before she found the treasure and stepped on the lily pad?

   a. 35
   b. 45
   c. 130
   d. 150

2. A waiter earned $75 on Saturday and $47 on Sunday. Then, he earned the same amount of money the next weekend. Which statement explains how to find the total amount of money the waiter earned both weekends?
   a. multiply 75 by 2, then add 47
   b. multiply 47 by 2, then add 75
   c. add 75 and 47, then multiply by 2
   d. add 75 and 2, then multiply by 47

3. Walker earns $12 for every lawn he rakes. He rakes exactly three lawns each day he works. Walker earned $288 last month. How many days did Walker work last month?
   a. 4 days
   b. 8 days
   c. 24 days
   d. 36 days

4. A national park plans to purchase a T-shirt for each of its 1,194 park employees and 783 park rangers. The cost per shirt is $5. Janet says that it would cost $18,855 to purchase the shirts. Which expression can best be used to decide whether Janet's answer is reasonable?

 a. (700 + 1,000) × 5
 b. (800 + 1,200) × 5
 c. (780 + 1,190) × 10
 d. (800 + 1,200) × 10

LESSON 1.4 ACTIVITY
Pattern Pandemonium

Directions: Complete the steps below.

1. Pick a card from the deck. This number is your starting number, and it will become the first number in your sequence.

2. Pick a second card from the deck. You will need to multiply your starting number by the number on the second card.

3. Pick a third card from the deck. You will need to add the number on this card to the product of the starting number and the second card. The sum of these two numbers will be the second number in your sequence.

4. Continue multiplying the latest number in the sequence by the second card and add that product to the third card in order to continue the sequence. Continue the sequence until the first 5 positions in the sequence is filled. Record your sequence on a note card.

5. Once you have the first 5 positions in the sequence, check your work with a calculator.

6. Swap your note card sequence with a partner for them to solve. You need to solve your partner's sequence and record the pattern in the space provided below.

    My partner's pattern:

Extend Your Thinking

1. Instead of adding the third card to the product of the first and second card, subtract the third card from this product and recreate the pattern.

LESSON 1.4 PRACTICE
Factor Pairs and Multiples

Directions: Complete the problems below.

1. The charts below tell the total number of crickets eaten by Mr. Moree's class's bearded dragon and Mrs. Nabors's class's tarantula.

Mr. Moree's Class's Bearded Dragon		
Day	Operation	Crickets Eaten
1		6
2		10
3		14
4		18
5		22
6		26
7		30

Mrs. Nabors's Class's Tarantula		
Day	Operation	Crickets Eaten
1		3
2		5
3		7
4		9
5		11
6		13
7		15

a. Will at any day the number of crickets eaten by both pets be the same? If so, explain using words and pictures or an algebraic operation to describe which day. If not, explain using words and pictures why there would not be a day in which the number of crickets eaten will be the same.

b. Predict how many crickets both animals will have eaten after 30 days. Create an algebraic operation that will fit in each chart under the column "Operation" in order to help support your prediction. Use a formula to do so.

2. Cora drew the following pattern using toothpicks:

She said her pattern increases the number of toothpicks used by 3 each time because a new triangle is added.

a. Is Cora's conclusion that adding 3 each time correct? Explain why or why not using words or pictures.

b. How many toothpicks are used in the first position? _____

c. How many toothpicks are added in each subsequent position? _____

d. Using your knowledge from Parts B and C, write an expression for Cora's pattern. _____

e. Based on the expression for this pattern, determine the number of toothpicks used in the 10th position in the space provided below.

3. Determine a rule using an expression that best represents the pattern seen below:

    a. Write your pattern in the space provided below.

    b. Explain why this rule works using words.

    c. Based on the expression, how many blocks would be in the 21st pattern? _____

4. Develop a shape pattern or number pattern that could follow both of the rules below. Be sure to extend the pattern to the sixth spot to make sure your pattern works.

$$(n \times 2) + 1 \qquad\qquad 2 + (n \times 3)$$

Extend Your Thinking

1. Examine a pinecone. Describe the number or shape pattern you may see in this object.

2. Research a number of shape patterns that occur naturally in nature and share them with your class.

LESSON 1.4

Assessment Practice

Directions: Complete the problems below.

1. Use the pattern to answer the question.

What letters show the type of pattern?

    a. AB AB
    b. AAB AAB
    c. AABB AABB
    d. ABB ABB

2. Justin knows that there are 4 wheels on a wagon. He wants to find the number of wheels on 6 wagons. Which number pattern should he use to find the answer?
    a. 4, 6, 8, 10, 12, 14
    b. 4, 8, 12, 16, 20, 24
    c. 6, 10, 14, 18, 22, 26
    d. 4, 10, 16, 22, 28, 34

3. Ann helps her mom decorate cookies. She puts 5 candies on each cookie. Ann wants to find the number of candies on 4 cookies. Which number pattern should Ann use?
    a. 4, 8, 12, 16
    b. 4, 9, 14, 19
    c. 5, 9, 13, 17
    d. 5, 10, 15, 20

4. Use the table below to answer the question. Heidi makes bracelets for a craft fair. Every day she makes 5 bracelets. She uses the table to record the total number of bracelets she has made. By Monday she has made 15 bracelets. Which statement will describe the number pattern of the table when it is completed?

Day	Monday	Tuesday	Wednesday	Thursday	Friday
Total Number of Bracelets	15	20			

    a. Every number in the pattern will divide evenly by 2 because 2 and 3 make 5.

    b. Every number in the pattern will divide evenly by 15 because 15 is the first number in the pattern.

    c. Every other number in the pattern will divide evenly by 10 because 5 and 5 make 10.

    d. Every other number in the pattern will divide evenly by 3 because 15 can be divided by 3.

LESSON 2.1 ACTIVITY
Jewelry Jinx

Directions: Mr. Daniels was getting ready to open his jewelry store one morning when an alarm went off on a car outside his shop, frightening him so much that he dropped the whole tray of rings he was carrying to the display case. The price tags on all of the rings (as seen in the table) fell off as they dropped to the floor. Mr. Daniels did not have a record of the prices he was charging for each ring; he only had the following clues:

- Ring A had a digit in the ones place that was 10 times less than the digit in the tens place for Ring C.
- Ring E had a digit in the tens place that was 10 times greater than the digit in the ones place for Ring G and 10 times less than the digit in the hundreds place for Ring C.
- Ring D had a digit in the ones place that has the same value as the digit in the ones place of Ring G.
- Ring A and Ring B have the same value in the ones place. Ring A and Ring F have the same value in the tens place.
- Ring C has a digit in the ones place that is 10 times less than the digit in the tens place for Ring F and 100 times less than the digit in the thousands place in Ring D.

Price Tags for Rings

$3,215	$531	$523	$153	$32	$15	$2

1. Using the clues and the prices in the table, match the rings to the correct price.

   a. Ring A: _____

   b. Ring B: _____

   c. Ring C: _____

   d. Ring D: _____

   e. Ring E: _____

   f. Ring F: _____

   g. Ring G: _____

2. Help Mr. Daniels organize his rings to best place them in his display case according to value. Use the following symbols (>, <, or =) to help him order his rings from least expensive to most expensive.

3. Mr. Daniels is worried that an incident like this might happen again and would like more clues just to be safe. Work with your partner to help Mr. Daniels develop more clues to match the rings to the correct price (please use place value understanding and comparisons when making these new clues). Write your clues on a separate sheet of paper.

4. Create a sign on a separate sheet of paper for Mr. Daniels to hang outside his store showcasing at least three of his items. Be sure to include the numeral form, expanded form, and written form for the three items he wants to showcase. He also wants to be able to show the multiplicative comparisons between place value positions, so consider this when choosing your items.

Extend Your Thinking

1. When Mr. Daniels was putting away his items at the end of the day, he accidentally spilled his water on the price tags for his rings, causing all of the ink to blur. Because all of the price tags are now illegible, he needs to create new price tags. Mr. Daniels is OK with this because he has wanted to raise his prices anyway. Work to create a new set of price tags that would raise the prices of each ring while allowing the clues to still work for each.

   a. Ring A: _____

   b. Ring B: _____

   c. Ring C: _____

   d. Ring D: _____

   e. Ring E: _____

   f. Ring F: _____

   g. Ring G: _____

LESSON 2.1 PRACTICE
Place Value Positions

Directions: Complete the problems below.

Nehemiah found the average salaries for different positions in the National Football League as seen in the table below.

Position	Average Salary in the NFL
Quarterback	$3,840,017
Cornerback	$1,690,105
Kicker	$1,662,786
Offensive lineman	$1,760,164
Running back	$1,550,624
Defensive end	$2,599,874
Linebacker	$1,803,388
Wide receiver	$1,806,999
Tight end	$1,420,890

1. What is the multiplicative relationship between the digit 6 in the average salary of a wide receiver and a cornerback?

2. Nehemiah said that he would rather be an offensive lineman than a wide receiver because he would rather make more money, as offensive linemen get 60 thousands while wide receivers only get 6 thousands. His friend Stone thinks something is not right with Nehemiah's reasoning. What do you think? Explain why you think this using expanded form to help support your thoughts.

3. Chastity was looking at the average salary of a quarterback and determined that 3 millions and 840 thousands is greater than $3,840,000. Do you agree or disagree? Explain why or why not using words.

4. Dillon was looking at the different positions to see which he should practice to possibly become a professional football player one day. He placed the salaries in order from least to greatest according to their expanded form to help him see the money he could make for each position. His work is shown below.

1,000,000 + 400,000 + 20,000 + 800 + 90
1,000,000 + 800,000 + 3,000 + 300 + 80 + 8
1,000,000 + 600,000 + 90,000 + 100 + 5
1,000,000 + 700,000 + 60,000 + 100 + 60 + 4
1,000,000 + 500,000 + 50,000 + 600 + 20 + 4
1,000,000 + 800,000 + 6,000 + 900 + 9
1,000,000 + 600,000 + 60,000 + 2,000 + 700 + 80 + 6
2,000,000 + 500,000 + 90,000 + 9,000 + 800 + 70 + 4
3,000,000 + 800,000 + 40,000 + 10 + 7

a. Dillon wants you to check over his work. Did he put these in the correct order from least to greatest? _____

b. Explain why or why not. Be sure to explain using expanded form for Dillon.

c. What do you think was Dillon's mistake in his ordering of the salaries?

Extend Your Thinking

1. Research the salary of some other profession (either another professional sport or a profession and its average salary across a number of states). What examples of multiplication relationships do you see when considering place value of certain digits?

LESSON 2.1
Assessment Practice

Directions: Complete the problems below.

1. Which expression does not represent 600? What number does it represent? _____
   a. 10 times 6 tens
   b. 100 × 6
   c. 10 × 60
   d. 10 groups of 6

2. Fill in the blank with the number that makes the equation true.

   4 ten thousands = _____
   a. 4 thousands
   b. 40 thousands
   c. 400 thousands
   d. 4,000 thousands

3. Which number is sixteen thousand four hundred seventy-two in standard form?
   a. 16,472
   b. 16,702
   c. 160,472
   d. 164,702

4. Sara saved $80 for a new toy. Her older sister had saved one hundred times as much money as Sara did for a new car. Which choice best answers how much money Sara's sister had saved?
   a. $80
   b. $800
   c. $8,000
   d. $80,000

LESSON 2.2 ACTIVITY
'Round the Box Office

Directions: Complete the steps below.

1. Using http://www.IMDB.com, research five of your favorite movies' opening weekend sales.

   a. Write these sales in the space provided below:

   Movie choice 1: _____ Sales: _____

   Movie choice 2: _____ Sales: _____

   Movie choice 3: _____ Sales: _____

   Movie choice 4: _____ Sales: _____

   Movie choice 5: _____ Sales: _____

   b. Using a number line, order these movies according to sales by rounding to the nearest million.

2. What is the difference between the highest grossing movie and the lowest grossing movie? Be sure to use the standard algorithm to show your work.

   Difference: _____

3. Calculate the sum of ticket sales of the top three movies. Be sure to use the standard algorithm to show your work.

Extend Your Thinking

1. Research the top 10 highest grossing movies of all time. Order these on a number line from least to greatest, rounding to the nearest 10 million. Then, total the sum of all of these movies using the standard algorithm.

2. Compare the total sum of the top 10 highest grossing movies to the average yearly income of a person in your home state (if you struggle finding this number, try comparing the sum to the population of your state, the average price of a new car, or the average price of a new house). How could this comparison help you understand more about economic concepts such as needs versus wants?

Total Sum: _____   Average Income: _____

LESSON 2.2 PRACTICE
Reasoning With Rounding

Directions: Complete the problems below.

1. For a social studies project, Jonas was researching the population of different counties in his state. Jonas decided that he would create a number line by rounding each county to the nearest thousand to help him compare the sizes.

County Name	Population
Lincoln County	47,082
St. Bernard County	41,567
Webster County	40,920
St. Martin County	52,728
Avoyelles County	41,569

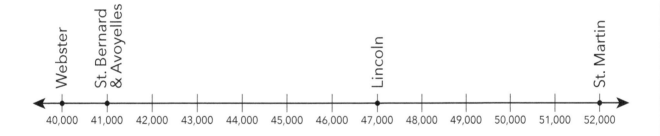

a. Is Jonas's number line reasonable? Explain why or why not. Draw a number line to help explain your answer.

b. Imagine that you needed to tutor Jonas on how to best use a number line to order a set of numbers by rounding to a certain place value. In the space below, write what you might say to him.

c. What is the difference between the number of people who live in St. Martin County and the number of people who live in Webster County? Please show your work using the standard algorithm.

2. Abi was looking at a hundreds chart and saw that any two-digit number with a number less than 5 in the ones place rounded down to the nearest ten and any two-digit number with a number greater than or equal to 5 in the ones place rounded up to the nearest ten. She thought that since this worked for all two-digit numbers, the same must be true for all three-digit numbers, except instead of rounding up or down to the nearest ten, it would round up or down to the nearest hundred. Do you agree or disagree with Abi's reasoning? Explain.

3. Graham is saving his money to buy a new laptop. The laptop he wants costs $539.99, and he has $42 saved already. Each week he receives $18 for helping out around the house with chores. He also collects cans for recycling and gets paid $1 per can. He usually can find around 26 cans a week. Estimate about how many weeks he will have to wait before he saves enough money to buy his laptop. Please explain your reasoning using both words and the standard algorithm for addition.

4. Determine which number line is the most reasonable for the problem stated below. Explain why.

Kris was drawing a number line to represent that he was 3/10 of the way toward earning the 8,300 points needed to win the big prize for end of the year banquet. He needs help deciding which number line is the most reasonable and most accurately shows 3/10 of 8,300.

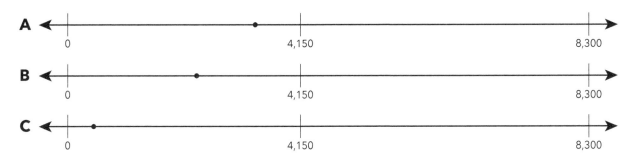

Extend Your Thinking

1. Research the population of 5–8 counties in your state and order them according to population size on a number line by rounding to the nearest ten thousand.

LESSON 2.2

Assessment Practice

Directions: Complete the problems below.

1. Ms. Robison wants to buy a boat. Ms. Robison rounds each boat price she sees to the nearest thousand. Which boat price rounds to $17,000?
   a. $16,479
   b. $17,089
   c. $17,532
   d. $18,777

2. Robbie lives in a town of 8,874 people. What is 8,874 rounded to the nearest thousand?
   a. 8,000
   b. 8,900
   c. 9,000
   d. 10,000

3. A school has 2,324 textbooks. Henry rounds this number to 2,000. What place value did Henry round to?
   a. ones
   b. tens
   c. hundreds
   d. thousands

4. 58,539 + 84,392 = _____

LESSON 2.3 ACTIVITY
Largest Possible Product

Directions: Complete the steps below.

1. Work with a partner to take turns drawing four cards from a deck.

2. Think strategically to create two 2-digit factors that will result in the largest possible product.

3. Check your partner's work by drawing an area array model on the dry erase board or loose-leaf paper to make sure their product is correct.

4. The person with the largest product wins.

5. Repeat Steps 1–4 for five rounds.

Extend Your Thinking

1. Draw six cards to create one 2-digit factor to multiply with a 4-digit factor to create a largest or smallest possible product. Check your partner's work by drawing an area array model.

2. With your cards you have already drawn, create least possible products.

3. Add in the ace cards, face cards, and 10 cards to practice multiplication with 3-digit factors.

LESSON 2.3 PRACTICE
Practicing With Products

Directions: Complete the problems below.

1. Imagine that you are going to open a lemonade stand with a friend for the summer. Below are some of the supplies you may need.
    *   Cups: packs of 24
    *   Lemonade mix: 1 package = 8 ounces
    *   Napkins: packs of 72

    a. You estimate that you will have around 225 customers this summer, based on sales from last summer. If you buy 11 packs of cups, will you have enough? Use an array area model to show your work.

    b. Would 11 packs of cups be a reasonable amount for you to buy based on your estimate? Why or why not?

    c. If you buy 136 packages of lemonade, how many ounces will you be able to make this summer? Draw an area model to show your work.

    d. If one pack of napkins cost $7, how much would you spend on napkins if you bought 4 packs? _____

2. Write the two factors that could produce the product 285 and also match the area model seen below. Explain your thinking by showing the decomposition of the two factors.

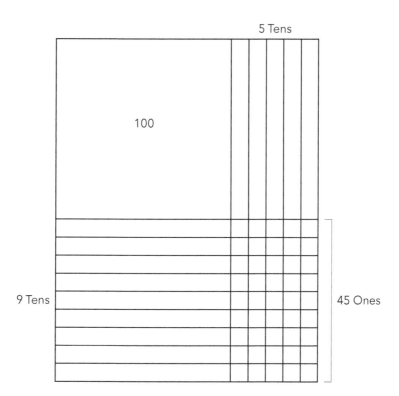

5 Tens

100

9 Tens

45 Ones

3. Olivia was using the standard algorithm to multiply two 2-digit factors. Her work is shown below. What mistake did Olivia make?

$$
\begin{array}{r}
43 \\
\times\,67 \\
\hline
2400 \ (40 \times 60) \\
280 \ (40 \times 7) \\
+\ \underline{180} \ (3 \times 60) \\
2{,}860
\end{array}
$$

4. Fill in the blanks to create a problem in which the product is a number that shows 8 hundreds. Explain why this works.

$$4 \times \underline{\hspace{1cm}}\,,\,2\,\underline{\hspace{1cm}}\ \underline{\hspace{1cm}}$$

Extend Your Thinking

1. Create your own problem like Number 2 or 4 of the practice to trade with a partner.

LESSON 2.3

Assessment Practice

1. There are 12 rows of seats in the school auditorium. Each row has 24 seats. The total number of seats can be found by evaluating the expression 12 × 24. How many seats are in the school auditorium?
   a. 24
   b. 36
   c. 72
   d. 288

2. Lela bought 6 boxes of cookies for the concession stand. Each box has 12 packs of cookies. How many packs of cookies did Lela buy in all?
   a. 2
   b. 8
   c. 66
   d. 72

3. Zachary Elementary School has 6 grades. There are 382 students in each grade. What is the total number of students in the school?
   a. 184,812 students
   b. 2,292 students
   c. 1,882 students
   d. 1,892 students

4. Four boys work together raking leaves. How much do they need to earn as a group for each boy's share to be $50?

LESSON 2.4 ACTIVITY
Let's Plan a Trip!

Directions: You want to convince your principal to take your grade level on a field trip. You can go anywhere in the country on your field trip. You need to research some information to present to your principal. The following items will help prepare you for your meeting with the principal.

Destination: _____

1. First, you need to determine how many miles it is to your destination. Research this using the map provided by your teacher. If you can only travel 300 miles a day, determine how many days this trip will take to travel there and back. _____

2. You need to charter buses that sit 52 people each. Determine the number of buses needed if all of the students in your grade, parents of half of the students, and one teacher for each class attends. _____

3. Each student and teacher will need a field trip shirt. Your school does not want to spend more than $6,000 on these shirts. If each student and teacher need a shirt, determine an estimated price for each shirt. _____

4. Each child and adult (parents and teachers attending) will need to eat. The school doesn't want to spend more than $4,000 on these meals. About how much should each meal cost? _____

Extend Your Thinking

1. If the school splits the field trip into three different trips, how much would each trip cost? Would this be better than taking everyone at once? Explain.

LESSON 2.4 PRACTICE
Produce Stand Division

Directions: Complete the problems below.

1. Your mom sent you to buy some fruit at the neighborhood produce stand. She wanted a 1-pound bag of apples and a 1-pound bag of oranges. However, the produce stand only sells 3-pound bags. You have managed to convince the owner to sell you a 1-pound bag each of apples and oranges under the condition you can calculate the cost of each bag and show him proof. The owner said you could use an area model to show your proof and round any decimals or fractions to the nearest cent.

   a. Calculate the cost of a 1-pound bag of apples if the 3-pound bag costs $2.98 (use cents only to calculate; i.e., $2.98 = 298 cents).

   b. Calculate the cost of a 1-pound bag of oranges if the 3-pound bag costs $4.43 (use cents only to calculate).

2. You want to bring an orange to school to split between you and your two friends. Your mom said that was OK as long as you paid her for the orange. You agreed, but want to make your friends pay for their share. You already found out in Question 1 how much your mom paid for the bag of oranges. You know that there are 7 oranges in the bag.

   a. Explain what math operation you would need to use to determine how much you need to pay your mom.

   b. Show your work using powers of ten to determine how much you need to pay your mom in cents for the orange.

   c. How much would the cost be if you equally split the price of the orange between you and your two friends? _____ Show your work using number disks.

d. Suppose you don't want to have to pay anything and instead want to make a profit of 61 cents. How much would each of your friends need to pay? _____ Explain your thoughts using words.

3. Mom wants to make apple pies for a bake sale and needs 128 apples. When you get to the produce stand, they have 3-pound bags that sell for $2.98. In each 3-pound bag, there are 6 apples.

   a. Determine the number of 3-pound bags Mom would need to make her apple pies. _____

   b. Mom wants to know if it would be more economical to buy an additional 3-pound bag or 2 single apples. Show your work to explain which choice would be cheaper.

4. You saw that mom was able to make 16 apple pies from her 128 apples and wondered how many apples went into each apple pie.

   a. What is the number of apples in each pie? _____

   b. Along with the information you already have, what else would you need to know if you were trying to determine the number of slices of pie? Tell how you would find the number of slices in one pie with this information.

Extend Your Thinking

1. Determine the number of slices you would need to cut each pie into if you wanted to have an even number of apples in each slice. _____

LESSON 2.4

Assessment Practice

Directions: Complete the problems below.

1. Evaluate: 805 ÷ 3
    a. 268
    b. 201
    c. 208 r 1
    d. 268 r 1

2. Mikie has 216 baseballs and 9 bags. She will put an equal number of baseballs in each bag. Which answer describes how the baseballs could be placed in the bags?
    a. There are 20 baseballs in each bag with 6 left over.
    b. There are 20 baseballs in each bag with none left over.
    c. There are 24 baseballs in each bag with none left over.
    d. There are 22 baseballs in each bag with 9 left over.

3. A store sells fishing lures in packages of 6. There are 488 individual lures in the store that need to be packaged. How many packages of lures can the fishing store sell?
    a. 81 packages
    b. 71 packages
    c. 98 packages
    d. 80 packages

4. A hotel has 8 floors with a total of 528 rooms. Each floor has the same number of rooms. How many rooms are on each floor?